Je

Monarch Child

Memoir poems

This book is dedicated to my beautiful boy.
I learn from you, I admire you, I love you.

Tell Upon Worlds, England, UK

First published in Great Britain by
Tell Upon Worlds *Micro Publisher* 2024
Typesetting and printing Amazon.com

ISBN 978-1-0685317-0-5

Author photograph © Booheads
Cover art © Jen If jen-if.co.uk

A CIP catalogue record for this book is available
from the British Library

"Behold, children are a heritage from the Lord,
the fruit of the womb, a reward."

PSALM 217:3

"Sit with me,
oh please, sit with me,
we'll take a moment to breathe..."

Song lyrics from 'Sit With Me' from the album 'Blazing' by
ALEXIA CHELLUN © 2024

With love for
every child who didn't make it,
those who somehow did,
and all those still trying.
Some of us are trying, for you.

Contents

Author's Note

These poems are written from memories of being trafficked out of the U.K. and into an organised programme of abuse. You may find them a distressing read.

It's difficult to know exactly how old I was but definitely younger than seven because I still had all my milk teeth. Many other children went through the same ordeal at the same time and it was clear that there had been many more before us. Some things we experienced include being drugged, electric shocks and hypnosis.

The poem *Art* relates to the same event I wrote about in *Gorgeous and Bleak* first published in Déraciné Literary Magazine, Volume IX, Summer 22. You can find it linked via my website.

If you're a survivor, these poems may be triggering. If you suspect you're a survivor but don't know, triggering is a dangerous process. If you decide to read this, do so with great caution and a skilled, trusted therapist.

Jen If

MONARCH CHILD

Like Mother, Like Daughter

Our matching eyes
of distant rain.
Remnants of sun through
her ever-shifting hair.

Vest and pants
in a scarlet case,
night dress and a squash-nosed bear,
like an overnight stay.

Did her hands overflow with love,
shame,
or lies,
when she passed that child,
to not-her-uncle?

Mother's Words

These are my mother's words.
Brew, ciggie, vehicle, yobbo, youths, wallop!
Knackers yard, like the clappers, phlegm, powers-that-be.
Hold your horses. Ye Gods! Kingdom Come.
Ratfink. Ratstails. Runt. Bitch.
What-can-I-do
and
No one will ever love you.

Words that sp-
lit and spit like scalding saliva.

The chief of these words?
Dirty.
Dirty.
Dirty.
As in: *The dog has done a*
and
You are.

The ones with the longest life?
What-can-I-do.
Not a question but
a statement of apathy,
a declaration of defeat,
a demand for absolution.

My mother gave me her words.
Ye Gods!
I'm learning another tongue.

Foldaway

Mother shrank.
When she picked me up,
my feet hung by her knees,
and my back was a question mark,
to keep my head near hers.

He was bigger than our world.
When he took me from her,
 - when she let me go -
I looked down on her.

Outside, a young woman,
her back a straining, bamboo rod,
felt like slow falling.
When shrugged to the ground,
I didn't know that I should run.

She folded me like old newspaper,
folded me in on myself,
folded me easily,
into the boot of her car.

Cold Clothes

Anorak, dog patch on pocket,
pastel dungarees,
cherry red jumper with silver thread,
crumpled plaid dress,
small, green bows.
Cardigan, embroidered sun,
pinafore and roll-neck set,
screwed-up gingham smock,
corduroy pants, rainbow belt,
suedette skirt,
half-petticoat.
Ladybird buttons.
Appliqué hearts.
T-shirts; Miffy, Muttley, Smurfette,
tangled tights with polka dots,
lace-trimmed ankle-socks,
assorted vests,
knickers with flowers,
creased, turquoise ribbon.

A steel barn, three quarters full,
of dark, dense layers,
congealed, bleak mounds,
stiff, damp heaps,
of bin bags,
of clothes.

gaps

in the disembodied black
am no
have no
in the disembodied black
dis bodied lack
of any
or any
and the words
and eyes no
no place no
not there
loud *smell*
a disconnect
roar
and *landslide*
fall
swift
cut drift

dis-bodied
all
suffer

> blink
> blink
> black

On the Second Day

Avoiding sticky walls,
girls pull on
the *week-a-day* pants
of strangers,
Thunderstorm Monday,
faded *Rainbow Friday*.

One needs to *go*,
but there's no water in the bowl.
She pees on dirt-dry ceramic,
where an Iron-bru can, old fags,
and small grasses grow.
Snapped chain, too high to reach,
she stretches,
tippy-toed on the rim of the seat.
It won't flush.
Grass at the bottom of an amber sea.

Long socks or tights over dappled thighs.
Most have never seen a kilt before.
They help each other.
    Are your buttons done right?
    What's your name, again?
The uniform has a hat, too -
they think they're being taken to a posh school.

A lady with teeth like ice,
plaits the hair of early finishers,
stroking the blondes.
Dampens a handkerchief,

scrubs oil off tender faces.

A slow dresser takes tiny steps,
to stop her *Foggy Tuesdays* falling down.
Later, at the airport,
a girl with angry tracks bisecting,
her torso from each leg,
will swap with her.

Now,
all the coats have been handed out,
she shivers at the back of the line,
thighs together.

Welcome

The noticeboard outside the chURch of SAinT AnN,
is a mess of capital and lower case letters,
poor nuns.
Thorns in their strip of garden might be roses,
have to look in daytime.
Hard to concentrate on what the head nun says,
obscured by her steam and smoke words,
the usual *do as you're told,*
we could have heard inside.
Light from church windows,
all the colours of warm,
licks rapt faces but
not me.
Thin sleeves,
dizzy head.

No Psychic Killer

Floating behind an overturned chair,
beige slacks, wadded arse up,
mushed cheeks concertina'd between tile,
and a white-shirt shoulder.
Your hands, all along,
tied behind your back,
point at the door.

You lied when you said
it was okay to call you names,
gave your permission,
said I had no choice, should forgive myself.
You paid in minutes; they quickly ushered me out.

Next door, in an office,
willing you strength,
cut as sharp as willing you dead.
I didn't know what to wish for.
An erratic needle wavered.

You gifted your cries at each blow.
Argued against assailants,
to let me know it wasn't me.
Your last act was love.

After,
I refused to step in your blood.

I could have bathed in it,
and only been made more pure.

She Sees the Smoke

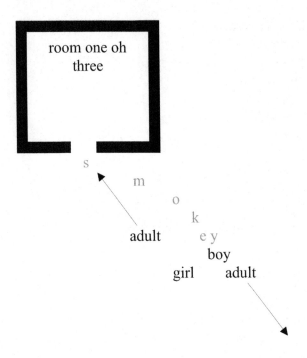

room one oh
three

s

m

o

k

adult   e y

boy

girl   adult

Helpless

White is an avalanche in a hall full of fog,
blown out lungs,
a breached, exposed underbelly.
White makes living things all shades of still-born.

White holds a mind under acid,

where,
it can't focus.

Blind white erodes sound,
ripens walls to glass
parts burst reaching through

shrunken seconds roll like marbles
stretch thoughts
sift
       paler
white

enters

Art

After dinner,
they pass the woman to stack their plates.
After stacking their plates,
they pass the woman to go to their dorm.
As they pass the woman,
hanging by the plates trolley,
as they pass the woman,
hanging by ropes,
as they pass the naked woman,
hung by the trolley,
the dripping woman,
they whisper to her,
because they are kind and because she's a woman,
as they'll be women,
whisper to the hung, cut and dripping woman,
> *If you get the chance, tell them you're sorry,*
> *next time, do as you're told,*
> *they need you to do what they say,*
> *do you hear, do you hear us?*
> *You have to do what they say.*
The cut woman hanging,
bleeds and drips but cannot speak,
and children go to their dorm.

The cut woman hanging,
bleeds and drips but cannot speak.
Children pass the woman to collect their plates.
After breakfast,
they pass the woman to stack their plates.

23 Seconds

She's almost at Theta.

Graphite words,
in downy brain bloom.
What have they been doing, down here?
Dive into the pink,
sink,
little tadpole with legs.

Oh, I'm losing her...

Pinker and pinker,
sea of subconscious.
Chimney smoke drifting.
Where is everybody?
In a town meeting.
Peek in the back door.

Bring her back up.

I am trying...

One, two, three, four,
Who's that knocking on my door?
Five six, seven, eight,
Hurry up, don't be late,
Nine, ten, eleven, twelve,
Gotta secret, I can't tell!

Yes, Theta.

19

Kicking down, against the pull of up,
caught on an electric hook.
A fat man, awkwardly, bloodily, face down,
who is responsible?
Oh, this is what they made me do.
No, this is what they made me think I did.
Pink fades to gentlest grey.
We know when to brace.

Delta.

Electrified fog for
one, two, three, four
hold on, it can only be for twelve seconds.

Increase the current.

Five, six,
seven, eight,
code prohibits more than twelve seconds

Already at legal maximum, Doctor.

nine, ten, eleven, twelve,

I said increase.

thirteen, fourteen, the bad man

But, Doctor, she could die.

fifteen, sixteen, he might not stop
seventeen uh uh senenteen

If she does, I'll make you pay because it's
your job to keep her alive.
I am the doctor and I make the decisions.

nineteentwenty tweny
one

twen two

twent

y th

r

e

e

The Woman Factory

Soft soled shoes,
rattling keys,
bars and clicking locks,
where grey men work.

Every head a red balloon,
that a child let go,
in an empty sky,
above a field of nodding poppies.

Wards full of slumber,
thoughts scoured,
words chemically removed,
little bodies prepped.

Squeak of heavy hooks along rails,
shoulders that barely bleed,
sighs of the not-living,
their closed-eyed stare.

One squirming chrysalis,
a long whistling scream
breaks like a brittle bone.
No-one stirs.
Secrets are dead-weight.

Small

Lower than a coffee table,
on my hands and knees.

Slight enough to put through a hatch,
in the back of a fuel truck,
pack in a suitcase,
or store under the floor.

Short enough to stand in a cupboard,
so the smiling man crouched,
to clip wrist, ankles, wrist,
elbows, waist, neck,
stainless bar across my chest,
before he shut the door,

but not quite thin enough,
so spikes punctured,
every time,
re-opening wounds,
every time,
punctured,
when he shut,
every time he,
shut the door.

So Over the Rainbow

caught the first ribbon sky blue dove grey peach blossom
aqua snaked on the breeze cloud white silver cotton candy
carnelian tick-a-tape monochrome mauve
steel a codified memory snow white rose red
poppy red of a captive daughter gunmetal shocking pink
amethyst the brush of cobweb sapphire plum
flesh water-blue satin, black velvet ghost
ruby red leather brown rope moonlight
raven wouldn't be trapped candy apple red
petrol blue slippery as air peacock
mist couldn't pin it down denim blue
orange tie it up or magic mint
ice blue let it go alice blue
liver bury the writhing shining ends crimson
charcoal deeply below jet black onyx
blood-red finger-skin numb and split army-green
bone bent under grey fatigue olive khaki
heliotrope eyes cast backwards purple
oxblood an ochre taste sepia
buff ignoring ribbons shadow
fawn of ash and gold cadet
dun blown round a crinkled neck lavender china-rose
tan stuck to knuckles avocado mud brown
fuchsia caught in hair ash grey
cadmium how I dug magnolia primrose
slate green ribbons underground bottle green
diamond cavern of earth roots and navy silk cornsilk
brick yellow subterranean cities emerald green
shell pink palaces, safe rooms golden
noir black scarf over my eyes sanguine

cloud white rag over my mouth almond
eggshell the need to collect and untangle alabaster
smoke breathe in eau-de-nil
platinum downpour from the clouds gilt
magenta inhaling streamers scarlet
raw umber puce vermilion teal artichoke
violet coiling in a raw viridian
open throat

Where the Words Hide

Bare-buttocked and trespassing,
tiptoe deeply,
down hallways of aged, amber doors.
Creamy, source-less light.
The roaring silence of movement, stopped.
The shrill-bell thickness of listening.

Doors to dawn and doors to dusk,
doors with handles,
doors hard locked.
Behind one of these you'll find the words,
a word, a mumble, a whimper.

A door ajar.
Autumn damp, mud-bald earth,
dying smoke and beer,
a bunker where you don't want to go.
No place for the child,
lying with her back to you.

Untie her ankles.
Dig the cord from her swollen neck.
Stroke your tears into her mottled arms,
and as she turns her blood-shot face to yours,
as you see her blood-shot face is yours,
will you swallow the scream you find in your mouth,
slam all the doors in the hallways of your mind?

For Graves

Witness
smoke etch doors on an autumn sky,
some or many.
Slip your winter hand from its glove,
reach through to melt, a little,
that solitary grief,
then gently swing the wide hurt shut.

Watch a sunset curdle.
See your prayer of a day unsaying itself,
vanish.

We, the Majority

Make-up artists. Kitchen staff. Orderlies. Computer and tech support. Science lab technicians. Animal handlers, esp. of dogs and chimpanzees. Employees of sensory floatation spas who shut naked children in, four to a tank. The man whose job it was to hang the ladder on the wall so it didn't catch fire. The foul-mouthed bus driver forced to surrender his half-drunk water. The kind student nurse I whispered I loved. The American lady with pink sweets and uncertain smile to whom I repeated and repeated my phone number. Bitter Joaquin, the janitor come cleaner, whose name meant *God will judge us,* who mopped, twice a day, congealed drips off a tiled floor under a work of *art.* Me. And now, you. All these people with the power to change the world.

Rain

My heart open,
navel to chin fills soft with drops of rain.
Floods blur the pages of my diary,
words bleed like ink from
a fountain pen that's leaked its last line,
and pages freed,
stick like flat, white moths to a window pane,
or spin a gentle ballet with each wave.
The flood in my heart drowns kittens in their sleep.
The weight of water breaks,
through papered walls of unremembered days.
Rain threads through me like silver veins.
Gentle deluge in a mother's throat,
a mid-breath, burbling,
     no,
open mouth and nose of water,
up-rushing bubbles bulge and shimmer.
Currents make rag-dolls of us.
A woman-stained sheet from her unmade bed,
tangles my legs slow-motion.
A coffee table meets her cheek,
sparks of teeth fly out like fireworks,
my head splits on old tile,
our water darkens, blue-black, thick red,
and long, tangled hair catches both our necks,
to choke old memories bursting to be shared.
Wash out this pain.
Fill me,
fill me with rain.

JEN IF is a writer diagnosed with autism. She is a survivor of ritual abuse (SRA), MC and sex-trafficking which she didn't escape until around the age of twenty-six. She has a bachelor's degree in English Literature and a Masters in Creative Writing. This is her first chapbook.

Printed in Great Britain
by Amazon